Spoddle

the

Frog

GBP.

First published 2020

Published by GB Publishing Org | www.gbpublishing.co.uk

Copyright ©2020 Holly Tillier

ISBNs

Paperback | 978-1-912576-91-3
eBook | 978-1-912576-92-0
Kindle | 978-1-912576-93-7

Designed by Holly Tillier

Written & Illustrated by Martyn Tillier

Dedication

This story is dedicated to my daughters Holly & Amy,
who heard it many years ago when they were little.
I hope it will help young children to read and inspire
them to make up stories of their own.

Spoddle the frog was a small green frog who lived in the pond at the end of Mrs Elderflower's garden. He was quite happy grubbing about in the weeds, leaves and mud in the lower parts of the pond, coming up for fresh air from time to time, sitting on the edge of the pond, enjoying the sunshine, then shading himself under some damp ferns, before jumping back into the cool water that was his home. He liked to dive down to the bottom to catch grubs and feed on the weeds, or sit up top, trying to catch insects, slugs and snails and other juicy delights that people tend to turn their noses up at.

Then one day his peaceful existence was shaken up by the sudden arrival in the pond of a plastic bag. This bag floated on the top for a while and had been put there by a large hand from one of the big people – probably Mr Elderflower. Inside the bag were three goldfish. They swam about in circles for some time, then gradually one by one they ventured out of the bag and started to dive and swoop through the water, racing each other to the bottom then back to the top, weaving among the lily stalks and chasing each other round and round their new home.

"Oh good," thought Spoddle, "at last some friends to play with. I hope they're nice and friendly."

But when he went over to say hello and introduce himself, they all suddenly turned away and looked down on him. One of them started to laugh in a gurgly fishy sort of way, came right up to him and said, "Ugh, what are you, and where did you come from? You must be a frog or a toad, I guess?"

The second one joined in, "You look disgusting and ugly, all green and spotty, not shiny and golden like us."

The third one swam beside him and flicked a fin at his leg, "Oh, and he's all slimy and warty. What a horrible thing you are. We're silky and smooth with lovely scales and sleek bodies. Look at how lovely we are compared to you... you... you frog!"

The three goldfish swam above him. "Oh, look how he's trying to swim, moving those leg things like a crawling insect and flapping those funny feet! We have perfect movement and balance just using our fins. Wouldn't you like to be like us? Look at what we can do."

The three of them treated Spoddle to a spectacular display of aquabatics, dashing in and out of the plants and finally ending up in a perfect line, all facing the friendly little frog and looking at him intently.

"There. What do you think of that?" asked the second fish with a smug sneer.

Spoddle thought for a moment and replied, "Yes, I can swim too, but I'd love to be able to swim the easy way you can. Do you think you could teach me?"

"Huh!" said the third fish, with a flick of its tail. "Don't be absurd! You wallow about and crawl through the water like some of the big people do. You will never be able to swim like us, and you're the wrong shape anyway!"

Not to be put off, Spoddle said, "But I can walk on the rocks and live among the leaves as well as in the water. How would you ever get out of the pond?"

"Why would we want to get out?" the first fish replied. "All we need to eat is here under the surface among the plants and lily pads."

Spoddle asked, "But wouldn't you like to sit on a lily pad and feel the lovely warm sunshine on your back?"

"Don't be ridiculous, you horrible little beast!" the second fish countered. "Sun indeed; it would dry out our skin and our scales might come off, and then we wouldn't look so beautiful."

"Yes," agreed the third. "And we are especially beautiful and attractive – so there."

Spoddle went on, "But if it gets too warm, I can either jump back into the pond, or if it rains, I can sit under a leaf and enjoy the lovely fresh soft rainwater on my back. I'm sure you'd like to do that, wouldn't you?"

The first fish cut him short...

"Nonsense, we are fish, not frogs. We are made to swim, not walk about, and anyway, your sunshine and rain sounds perfectly ghastly, so you'd better keep out of our way and catch your food up on the surface, because if there's anything yummy under the water, we'll soon get at it, so you'd better stick to your revolting insects and slugs and snails, ugh!"

With that said, they all dashed around sucking up the tiny bits of plant stuff and food in the water.

So Spoddle went down to the depths and sat for a while, feeling thoroughly miserable. He thought about moving to another pond, but he didn't know where the nearest one was and he might get terribly lost in the big gardens up above and never find one; then he would waste away without any water to live in.

And to make matters worse, there were big animals up there that often ate frogs and small creatures and he didn't much like the idea of being eaten. He was after all a fairly timid and shy creature. Perhaps, he thought, tomorrow the fish would be more used to their new home and would be more friendly towards him, and with that he went to sleep.

Next morning he woke up early, as the first light broke through the reeds from above. He swam up to the surface, hoping to get there without disturbing the goldfish, but they were already there, waiting for him to appear.

"So it's you again, is it frog?" the first one began. "We thought you would have got the message and gone away from here. We don't want your kind in our pond!"

"No, it lowers the tone of the neighbourhood having green creatures about," said the second. "We were brought here to improve the place, brighten it up, and add lots of colour. Look at how stunning we are, how beautiful and perfectly formed we are... oh, and we don't mix with lowly pond life."

After a couple of days of this, Spoddle had become quite upset. The fish would have fun chasing him around the pond; how he wished to be showy and bright like them, standing out against the grey-green water, rather than being hidden in it. How he wanted to be able to swim gracefully like them and not to have to use his arms and legs and work hard to get anywhere. But he had to face up to it. He wasn't like them and they were too haughty and snobbish to have anything to do with him, except laugh and show off. He had some company at last in the pond, but he'd never felt so alone.

Each day, the three fish would sport and play up near the surface of the water, trying to outdo each other with their swimming skills, even moving sideways and backwards, and challenging him to join in, so they could make fun of his awkwardness, his croaky voice, and his knobbly skin. They even made fun of his colour.

"Green, how perfectly dreadful, that's the colour of plants and the things we eat; it's not a proper colour for a fish! Look at us in our gold, orange and silver. Those are real colours, classy and sophisticated; not like green. That's the colour of slime and oooooze..."

Spoddle protested, "But I'm not a fish, I'm an amphibian." He was of course a well-educated amphibian at that. "I can't do fishy things, and if all the fish in the world are like you three, I don't want to be one either."

"Well, I've never been so insulted," said the second fish. "Let's ignore this common little green thing and go and show ourselves to the big ones up above. They don't have time to waste on frogs; they want to see beauty instead." And with that, they flounced off in a flurry of fins, in a way that only goldfish can.

Then one day there came a heron.

A very big white hungry heron, flying quite high up above the people's gardens, looking for a meal. It spotted the three shiny golden shapes moving about near the surface of the pond and decided to take a closer look...

Down below in the pond, the fish were unaware of this, especially as fish tend to look around and below them but seldom above. They were doing their usual thing, playing at splashing each other and showing off their beautiful shiny scales and their clever moves. Spoddle was rooting around in the vegetation near the bottom looking for scraps, and as usual the three fish were enjoying their daily game of taunting him.

"Found anything to eat yet, any worms or snails or nasty bits of weed then?" sneered the first fish.

The second continued, with a mean laugh: "I think he's getting thinner. Never mind – we aren't!"

The third fish performed an acrobatic somersault and dived down close to Spoddle, flicking him with its tail, then shot up towards the surface crying out, "Look at me – I can do this! I bet you wished you were as fast as me."

But as Spoddle looked up at them, he noticed something high up above the water, something big and white with wings, something that was circling around and getting closer and closer. "Look out!" he cried. "There's a..."

Then all of a sudden it disappeared. The fish looked about and up at the sky, but there was nothing there.

"Stupid frog trying to scare us, go back to the depths where you belong," said the second fish.

Spoddle replied, "But I saw a bird, a very big bird."

The fish went on, "You're imagining it. Anyway, it's time we played chase the frog," and with that, all three chased him away then swam up towards the surface.

They did not see that the heron had landed next to the pond, and was standing away from the water's edge so it couldn't be seen. If it had lips, which it didn't, it would have been licking them. In fact, its beady eyes were following every move they made, as it stood absolutely still, watching...

"Come on," said the third fish. "Forget the silly frog and let's have a race around the lily pads!"

That moment, the heron's massive beak hit the water and opened up like a cavern. It swept up the three goldfish in its mouth and with one great gulp, swallowed them all.

GULP!!!

Just like that! A terrified Spoddle made himself as small as possible in the weeds, not daring to move a muscle, not daring to let out a tell-tale bubble of air, in case the bird fancied dessert.

Fortunately for our green hero, the heron hadn't noticed him camouflaged against the rotting leaves in the gloomy and dark pit of the pond and so, after letting off a huge fishy-flavoured burp, it flew away.

It was some time before Spoddle ventured out of his hiding place. The pond suddenly felt much bigger now the fish were gone, and quieter, but also a lot scarier. He decided not to go up to the surface until it got dark, so next morning having carefully breakfasted on the rocks, on a snail and a few flies, he gradually began to feel a bit happier. He realised that although he wasn't gold- or silver-coloured, perhaps green wasn't such a bad colour to be after all.

He was a perfectly good swimmer and he didn't actually want to show off much, and he quite liked his healthy diet of slugs and snails and insects. In fact, he was suddenly happy to be a frog! He felt a bit sorry for the fish, but that soon wore off, and he got back to his daily routine of searching for food above the water, but always wary of big birds and other animals that might fancy some delicious frog's legs for their tea.

The next day, Spoddle was sitting on a rock by the pond when the big people came by. He slid under a leaf and watched as they scratched their heads wondering where the fish had gone. "Probably a heron," said Mrs Elderflower. "We'll have to put a net over it if we get some more fish."

"Yes, I suppose so," said her husband. "Unless we keep newts and frogs instead, or tench. They're a sort of grey-green and wouldn't be spotted so easily."

Mrs Elderflower frowned. "But that's a bit boring. Much as I like newts and toads and so on, they're all a bit dull. I like a good colourful show. Oh look!" she suddenly said, "there's a cute little frog."

Spoddle thought he'd been seen and just to be safe, he dived off the rock, splashed into the water and swam towards the bottom. But it wasn't him that Mrs Elderflower had seen. There was another frog down there among the leaves...

"Hello, I'm Spoddle. Who are you?" he asked of the newcomer.

"I'm Despina, and I'm looking for a new home. I come from another pond a few gardens away, and the big ones have put some rather grumpy Koi carp in recently, and the place is a bit crowded and just not the same anymore. Can I stay here with you please? It's nice and cosy here."

Despina fluttered her eyelids, which Spoddle thought were a particularly lovely shade of green.

Spoddle thought for a moment, wondering why fish had to be so awkward, unlike frogs, toads and newts. It would be nice to be able to share the pond with a friend, especially a girl frog.

"But are you sure you want to live with a croaky, green creature like me?" he asked her.

Despina smiled a specially-wide froggy smile. "Well, you look perfectly alright to me, so what do you think – can I stay?"

Suddenly Spoddle felt very happy. "Just as long as you won't get bored. You see, nothing ever happens much around here. But of course you can stay. I hope you like it. It is a nice place."

The End

Look out for further adventures of Spoddle the Frog;

- Spoddle & Despina meet the tenches

- The pond gets connected to the net

- The splishy splash of tiny tadpoles

- Nancy the Nanny Newt comes to stay

www.ingramcontent.com/pod-product-compliance
Lightning Source LLC
Chambersburg PA
CBHW051242020426
42331CB00016B/3483